MA~

HOLLYWOOD

JESUS

A SMALL GROUP STUDY
CONNECTING CHRIST AND CULTURE

LEADER GUIDE
WRITTEN BY JOSH TINLEY

Abingdon Press / Nashville

HOLLYWOOD JESUS
LEADER GUIDE
BY JOSH TINLEY

A SMALL GROUP STUDY
CONNECTING CHRIST AND CULTURE

This book is printed on elemental chlorine-free paper.
ISBN 978-1-5018-0393-2

15 16 17 18 19 20 21 22 23—10 9 8 7 6 5 4 3 2 1
MANUFACTURED IN THE UNITED STATES OF AMERICA

CONTENTS

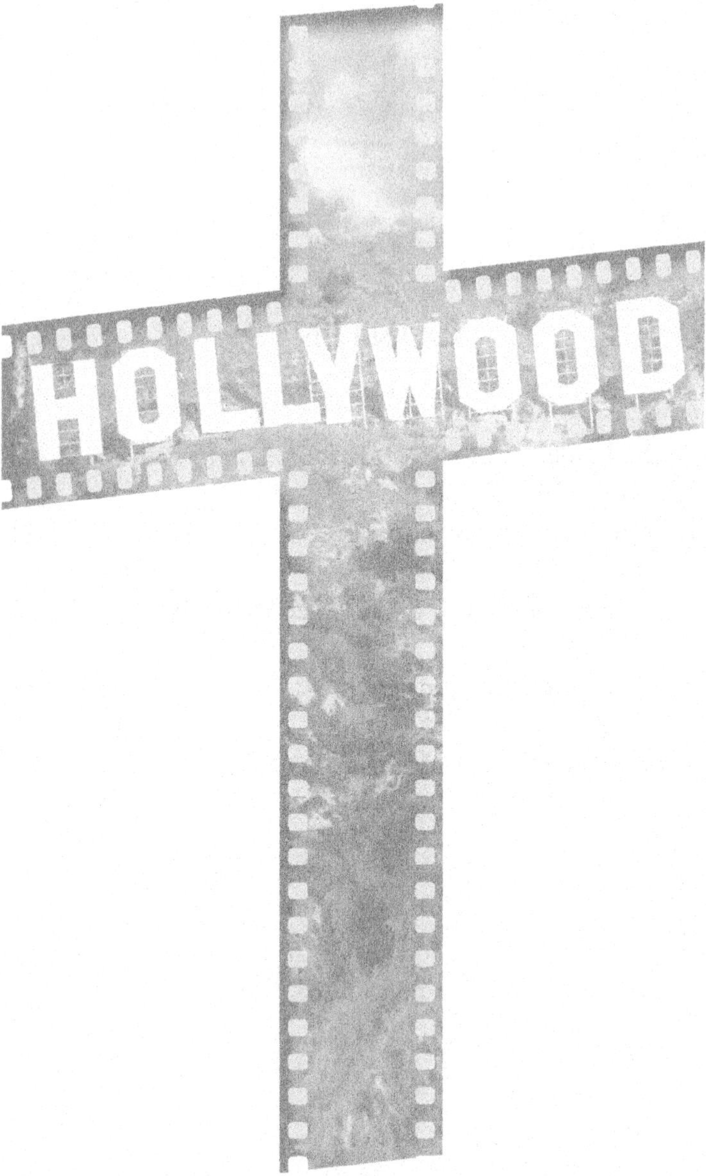
HOLLYWOOD

TO THE LEADER

This Pop in Culture Bible study series is a collection of studies about faith and popular culture. Each study uses a work or medium of pop culture as a way to examine questions and issues of the Christian faith. Studies consist of a book, DVD, leader guide, and worship resources flash drive. Our hope and prayer is that the studies will open our eyes to the spiritual truths that exist all around us in books, movies, music, and television.

As we walk with Christ, we discover the divine all around us, and in turn, the world invites us into a deeper picture of its Creator. Through this lens, we are invited to look at culture in a new and inviting way. We are invited to dive into the realms of literature, art, and entertainment to explore and discover how God is working in and through us and in the world around us to tell his great story of redemption and hope.

For more than a century, film has been one of the most popular and prominent mediums for art and entertainment. And for more than a century, filmmakers have looked to Scripture—and particularly the story of Jesus found in the Gospels—for stories and material. Jesus first took to the big screen in the 1903 French silent film *La vie et la passion de Jésus Christ* ("The Life and Passion of Jesus Christ") and has returned dozens of times since. Some of these portrayals of Christ became classics, some were controversial, and some just plain bombed with audiences. Regardless, Hollywood's take on our Lord and Savior has certainly had an impact on our culture and our understanding of Jesus.

In his book *Hollywood Jesus,* author and pastor Matt Rawle examines many of the ways in which moviegoers have encountered Jesus over the years. He looks at some of cinema's most famous Jesus movies, such as *Ben-Hur, Jesus of Nazareth,* and *The Passion of the Christ.* But he also sees Jesus in films without a biblical setting, such as *Star Wars, WALL-E, Cool Hand Luke,* and *Monsters, Inc.* Participants in this study will consider these movies and several others, reflecting on what we can learn from the Jesus of Hollywood and how film can be a medium for spreading the gospel message.

How to Facilitate This Study

Participants in this study do not need to have seen any of the movies discussed. They will have opportunities to discuss where they have seen Christ in the movies they know and love. That said, you may get more out of this study if participants have some familiarity with the movies Rawle discusses. As you prepare for this study, encourage participants to check out some of these movies:

- *Ben-Hur*
- *Jesus of Nazareth* (miniseries)
- Monty Python's *Life of Brian*
- The Star Wars trilogies
- The Lord of the Rings trilogy

- *WALL-E*
- *Cool Hand Luke*
- *Monsters, Inc.*

This four-session study makes use of these components:

- the study book, *Hollywood Jesus* by Matt Rawle
- this Leader Guide
- *Hollywood Jesus* DVD

You will need a DVD player or computer, and a television or projection screen so that you can watch the DVD segments as part of your group session. Participants in the study will also need access to Bibles during the session; many activities will also require basic supplies including a markerboard or large sheets of paper and markers, pens and pencils, and index cards and/or slips of paper.

Each session is structured into a 60-minute format:

- Opening Activity and Prayer (10–15 minutes)
- Watch DVD Segment (10 minutes)
- Study and Discussion (30–35 minutes)
- Closing and Prayer (5–10 minutes)

If you have more time in your session, or want to utilize other activities during your session, "Additional Options for Bible Study and Discussion" are included for each chapter, listed after the closing prayer.

HELPFUL HINTS

Preparing for Each Session

- Pray for wisdom and discernment from the Holy Spirit, for you and for each member of the group, as you prepare for the study.
- Before each session, familiarize yourself with the content. Read the study book chapter again.
- Choose the session elements you will use during the group session, including the specific discussion questions you plan to cover. Be prepared, however, to adjust the session as group members interact and as questions arise. Prepare carefully, but allow space for the Holy Spirit to move in and through the group members and through you as facilitator.
- Prepare the space where the group will meet so that the space will enhance the learning process. Ideally, group members should be seated around a table or in a circle so that all can see one another. Moveable chairs are best, so that the group can form pairs or small groups for discussion easily.

Shaping the Learning Environment

- Create a climate of openness, encouraging group members to participate as they feel comfortable.
- Remember that some people will jump right in with answers and comments, while others need time to process what is being discussed.
- If you notice that some group members seem never to be able to enter the conversation, ask them if they have thoughts to share. Give everyone a chance to talk, but

keep the conversation moving. Moderate to prevent a few individuals from doing all the talking.

- Communicate the importance of group discussions and group exercises.
- If no one answers at first during discussions, do not be afraid of silence. Count silently to ten, then say something such as, "Would anyone like to go first?" If no one responds, venture an answer yourself and ask for comments.
- Model openness as you share with the group. Group members will follow your example. If you limit your sharing to a surface level, others will follow suit.
- Encourage multiple answers or responses before moving on to the next question.
- Ask, "Why?" or "Why do you believe that?" or "Can you say more about that?" to help continue a discussion and give it greater depth.
- Affirm others' responses with comments such as "Great" or "Thanks" or "Good insight"—especially if it's the first time someone has spoken during the group session.
- Monitor your own contributions. If you are doing most of the talking, back off so that you do not train the group to listen rather than speak up.
- Remember that you do not have all the answers. Your job is to keep the discussion going and encourage participation.

Managing the Session

- Honor the time schedule. If a session is running longer than expected, get consensus from the group before continuing beyond the agreed-upon ending time.
- Involve group members in various aspects of the group session, such as saying prayers or reading the Scripture.

- Note that the session guides sometimes call for breaking into smaller groups or pairs. This gives everyone a chance to speak and participate fully. Sometimes the study gives instructions for grouping participants. In other cases, mix up the groups; don't let the same people pair up for every activity.
- As always in discussions that may involve personal sharing, confidentiality is essential. Group members should never pass along stories that have been shared in the group. Remind the group members at each session: confidentiality is crucial to the success of this study.

Session 1

FROM SCRIPTURE TO SCRIPT

PLANNING THE SESSION

Session Goals

Through this session's discussion and activities, participants will be encouraged to:

- reflect on the role that story plays in the church;
- consider how stories point to truths beyond themselves;
- look at the ways they tell Jesus' story;
- identify the essential truths about Jesus that God calls us to communicate;
- examine how we fill in the spaces in Jesus' story, and how these filled-in spaces affect our understanding of Jesus;
- consider, referring to Mark 12:30, the different ways that Christians receive the gospel story: heart, mind, soul, and strength.

11

Preparation

- Read and reflect on the first chapter of Matt Rawle's *Hollywood Jesus.*
- Read through this Leader Guide session in its entirety to familiarize yourself with the material being covered.
- Read and reflect on the following Scriptures:
  - ❏ Philippians 2:5–11
  - ❏ Matthew 14:13–21
  - ❏ Matthew 21:12–17
  - ❏ Mark 1:16–20
  - ❏ Luke 10:38–42
  - ❏ John 12:1–11
  - ❏ John 20:24–29
  - ❏ Romans 14:14–23
  - ❏ Mark 12:30
  - ❏ Matthew 4:1–11
  - ❏ Matthew 8:5–13
  - ❏ Matthew 8:23–27
  - ❏ Matthew 21:12–17
  - ❏ John 4:4–30
  - ❏ John 11:1–46
- Make sure that you have a markerboard or large sheet of paper on which you can record group members' ideas.
- Have a Bible for every participant.
- Have a sheet of paper and a pen or pencil for each participant. Other art supplies are optional for the closing activity.

OPENING ACTIVITY AND PRAYER
(10–15 MINUTES)

The title of a popular 1965 film called the life, death, and resurrection of Jesus *The Greatest Story Ever Told*. While Christians largely consider Jesus' story singularly great, all of us have encountered other great stories, whether on film or in print.

To open your time together, ask each participant to name a story he or she would consider "great." These stories can be from movies, novels, short stories, television, comic books, or oral. They can be fictional stories or true stories, but they should be stories that have some special meaning to the participant who chooses them.

After everyone has had time to respond, list these on a markerboard or large sheet of paper. Once you've made your list, ask:

- What stories were you surprised made our list? Why?
- What are some common themes you notice in these stories?
- Why do you think people are drawn to these stories?
- Introduce the topic of this study: portrayals of the gospel through film. Then ask:
- Which of the stories on our list bear similarities to Jesus' story?
- What makes Jesus' life, death, and resurrection so compelling as a story?

Lord, thank you for bringing us together to examine the ways we hear and tell your story, particularly through film. Watch over us these next few weeks as we explore Jesus' life and ministry from different perspectives. Thank you for the

*different gifts, experiences, and points of view each person
brings to this group. May we take what we learn during our
time together and use it more effectively to tell Jesus' story to
those who are eager to hear it or who need to hear it in new
ways. Amen.*

WATCH DVD SEGMENT
(10 MINUTES)

STUDY AND DISCUSSION
(30–35 MINUTES)

<u>Note:</u> Discussion helps and questions that correspond to
Chapter One: "From Scripture to Script" are provided below. If
you have more time in your session, or want to include additional
discussion and activities to your time, see "Additional Options
for Bible Study and Discussion" at the end of this section, listed
after the Closing Activity and Prayer.

How to Tell a Great Story
(See *Hollywood Jesus*, pages 23–27)

Revisit the list of great stories that participants compiled for
the opening activity. Rawle writes that great art "points beyond
itself." In other words, great stories make a point or have some
significance beyond the events of the story itself.

Ask each participant to select one story from the list you
compiled earlier and to say how it points beyond itself. For
example, if the *Harry Potter* saga was on your list, a participant
might say that it teaches lessons about courage, sacrifice, love,
and humility. If *Animal Farm* is on the list, a participant might

mention that this story is an allegory of Soviet Communism under Stalin. (You might also refer to Rawle's example of "The Three Little Pigs" on pages 23–24.)

Then read what Rawle writes on pages 24–25 about how the story of the gospel points beyond itself.

For discussion:

- How does the gospel point to something beyond itself?
- How is the gospel more than just another great story?
- What do you think Rawle means when he says that the gospel cannot "be contained within a category on Netflix"?

The Space Between

(See *Hollywood Jesus*, pages 31–36)

Read aloud Rawle's assessment of the classic miniseries *Jesus of Nazareth* on pages 31–32, focusing on how the creators of the series filled in spaces where Scripture itself was silent. To get a feel for the challenges the filmmakers faced, divide participants into teams of three or four and assign each team one of the following Scriptures:

- Matthew 14:13–21
- Matthew 21:12–17
- Mark 1:16–20
- Luke 10:38–42
- John 12:1–11
- John 20:24–29

Each team should read its assigned Scripture with an eye on the "spaces in between." Teams should think of ways to fill in these spaces. For example, John 12:1–11 gives the impression that Jesus' disciples are present. But, except in the case of Judas, the text doesn't say anything about how his disciples responded to Mary pouring out ointment on Jesus' feet. This is a space that we are left to fill in.

After teams have had plenty of time to read, discuss, and fill in the spaces of their Scriptures, invite each team to summarize its passage, name the spaces identified, and say how these spaces might be filled. Following each team's presentation, ask participants what surprised them about how that team filled in the spaces of its Scripture.

Read aloud or summarize for the group:

Even when Christians are not piecing together the parts of the narrative on the margins of the stories in Scripture, we're filling in spaces in the Bible. As Rawle points out, the Bible doesn't give us specific instructions for responding to any situation imaginable. We have spaces to fill in. For that we must rely on the guidance of the Holy Spirit.

For discussion:

- How do you experience the Holy Spirit's presence and guidance?
- How do you seek counsel from the Holy Spirit when making a decision, particularly a decision you must make quickly?

As a group, read what the apostle Paul writes in Romans 14:14–23. Discuss:

- What does Paul teach us in these verses about living in the Holy Spirit?

16

- What does Paul teach in these verses about filling in the spaces in Scripture?
- What is most challenging about following the guidance of the Holy Spirit (as opposed to looking for a clear "yes" or "no" from Scripture)?

Framing Jesus
(See *Hollywood Jesus*, pages 36–40)

Read aloud or summarize for the group:

As Rawle explains in this section of *Hollywood Jesus*, storytellers—whether authors or filmmakers—frame their stories, creating a structure that allows the story to take place. He notes the opening words of Genesis and the final verses of Revelation frame the Bible as one giant prayer.

Jesus' story is told in each of the four Gospels. Compare and contrast how each of the Gospels frames its story. As a group, look at the Gospels one at a time, looking at the opening verses, then skimming the first chapter and the last chapter, focusing on the final verses. (Keep in mind that Mark has two different endings, a short one that is most likely the original ending and a longer one that was probably added later.) After going through all four, discuss:

- What differences do you notice in the ways that the Gospel writers frame their stories?
- Why do you think the different Gospel writers choose different starting and ending points?
- What does the way each Gospel is framed say about the writer's intent and point of emphasis?

Rawle goes on to discuss how filmmakers frame not only stories but individual shots. He also covers how different Hollywood portrayals of Jesus frame Jesus in different ways.

For discussion:

- Why do you think the Bible gives us four accounts of Jesus' life, each framed in a different way?
- How can the different portrayals of Jesus on film—even ones whose accuracy we doubt—help us better understand who Jesus is and why he is important?
- Of the Hollywood depictions of Jesus that you are familiar with, which have had the biggest impact on your understanding of Jesus? How did the makers of these films frame Jesus' story?

CLOSING ACTIVITY AND PRAYER
(10 MINUTES)

As Hollywood filmmakers prepare to shoot a movie, they usually create a storyboard. A storyboard is a set of comic book-style panels or sheets of paper, each of which contains a rough sketch of one scene of the film. Storyboards are helpful for organization and sequencing and make clear how the visuals of the film connect to the script.

To close your time together, give each participant a sheet of paper and instruct him or her to create a storyboard panel illustrating one scene from Jesus' life that you looked at during this session. Through drawings or words, participants should consider how they will frame the scene, what they will focus on, what characters will be in the scene, and what the setting will look like. (If your group is large, you may want to break into teams for the sake of time.)

Give participants plenty of time to work, then post their storyboard panels in your meeting space. As possible, arrange the panels in story order. Have each person talk about:

- What "scene" he or she chose.
- Why he or she chose this scene.
- What he or she hopes this scene will explain to an audience about Jesus.

Close your time together by discussing the following:

- What aspects of Jesus' story resonate most with you? Why?
- Based on what we've discussed today, how can film help us better understand and appreciate Jesus' story?
- Could film ever distort or hinder our understanding of Jesus?
- What is one thing you learned or realized about Jesus from this session that you didn't know or realize before?
- In what ways do you tell Jesus' story? How will what we've discussed today affect how you communicate Jesus' story? What might you take into consideration that you wouldn't have otherwise?

Lord, thank you for this time we've had together. Thank you for living among us as Jesus, giving us the "greatest story ever told." You have called and equipped us to be storytellers. Give us the vision and wisdom to be aware of all the ways we tell your story, to be mindful of how others perceive the story we tell, and to find new ways to tell the good news of Jesus. In his name we pray, amen.

ADDITIONAL OPTIONS FOR BIBLE STUDY AND DISCUSSION

Decisions, Decisions (15 minutes)
(See *Hollywood Jesus*, pages 27–31))

Read aloud or summarize for the group:

Matt Rawle asks us to imagine giving a three-minute "elevator speech" about who Jesus is and why he is important. When we're short on time, we must use our words wisely. Rawle mentions Philippians 2:5–11 as an example of the apostle Paul giving a concise summary of Jesus' story and significance.

Activity:

Read Philippians 2:5–11. Based on these verses, as well as their prior knowledge about Jesus, have participants come up with a summary, in three minutes or less, of Jesus' life and significance. Have participants pair off. One person in each pair should give an elevator speech to his or her partner. Set a timer to make sure that these speeches don't exceed three minutes. After three minutes, have partners switch roles. Following this activity, ask:

- How effective do you think your summary was?
- What do you wish you had included that you didn't?
- Is three minutes enough time to adequately introduce someone to Jesus? Why, or why not?
- What do you think would be most challenging about writing and directing a movie about Jesus, particularly when it comes to deciding what to include and what to cut?

For discussion:

Rawle writes that we make decisions about how we portray Jesus not only when we tell his story but also through our words and actions. What do your words and actions reveal to people about Jesus?

- When and how might you have given someone the wrong impression of who Jesus is and what he means for us?
- How does our congregation tell Jesus' story in worship? What could we do better?
- Rawle warns against making Jesus in our own image. When have you confused Jesus' priorities for your own? How might this have given people a warped image of God?

A New Gaze (10 minutes)

(See *Hollywood Jesus*, pages 40–44)

Read aloud or summarize for the group:

Read the greatest commandment from Mark 12:30. This commandment echoes Deuteronomy 6:5, but Jesus changes the wording a little bit. The verse in Deuteronomy mentions loving God with our heart, soul, and being. The verse in Mark mentions heart, mind, soul (or being) and strength. Rawle uses Jesus' words in Mark 12:30 to examine the different ways that we, as members of an audience, receive the stories we hear.

Read through Rawle's description of heart, mind, soul, and strength people on pages 43–44. Then, as a group or in teams of four or five, read each of the following Gospel Scriptures and discuss whether each one would appeal most to a head, mind, soul, or strength person. (There is not necessarily one right or wrong answer for each of these.)

- Matthew 4:1–11
- Matthew 8:5–13
- Matthew 8:23–27
- Matthew 21:12–17
- John 4:4–30
- John 11:1–46

For discussion:

- Would you describe yourself as a heart, mind, soul, or strength person? Why?
- How might these differences in perspective and interpretation cause division in the church?
- How does the church benefit from having people of each type?

Activity: Pitch a Movie

Divide participants into teams of three to five. You can assign teams at random, group together people who all appreciate a particular movie genre, or create teams based on whether participants identify as heart, mind, soul, or strength people (see the previous "A New Gaze" activity).

Each team should come up with a pitch for a movie about Jesus' life. To begin, teams should consider the following:

- What do you want audiences to know about Jesus?
- What aspect(s) of Jesus' life and ministry do you want to focus on?

- How will you frame your story? How will the story open? What will its climax be? Its resolution?
- Will your story follow one of the four Gospels? Will it follow a particular series of events?
- In addition to Jesus, who will some of the primary characters be? Will your movie be told from a particular character's point of view?

Once teams have considered all of the above questions, they should create a rough outline of their movie idea. This outline doesn't need to use roman numerals and letters; rather it should be a series of 10–15 sentences and/or short paragraphs explaining the overall story arc and major plot points. Time may not allow teams to put together a complete outline. That's okay, as long as team members have an understanding of their movie's plot, key scenes, and points of emphasis.

After teams have had enough time to put their movie ideas together, have each team "pitch" its movie to the others. In their pitches, teams should summarize their movies using the outlines they've put together; they also should explain what makes their movie unique and what they hope the movie will communicate about Jesus.

Following each pitch, participants should act as producers. They should ask questions for clarification; they should identify things that they like about the idea; and they should give suggestions for ways to alter the story so that it more effectively communicates its intended message.

After all of the pitches, discuss:

- How would our movies be different from other Hollywood portrayals of Jesus?

- How might our movies reach people who were previously unfamiliar with Jesus' story or who had not heard Jesus' story in a way that resonated with them?
- Might any of our movies be controversial? If so, why?
- Do you think actual Hollywood producers would be interested in making a movie like those you've pitched? Why, or why not?
- How do you maintain a relationship with Christ amid the challenges, sacrifices, and dangers?

Session 2

THE JESUS OF NOW . . . WHENEVER "NOW" IS

PLANNING THE SESSION

Session Goals

Through this session's discussion and activities, participants will be encouraged to:

- evaluate how stories and accounts are products of a particular place and time;
- determine which qualities of Jesus are specific to the time and place in which he lived and which are timeless characteristics that we should emulate;
- name the assumptions they make about Jesus' identity and priorities;
- identify ways that they recreate Jesus in their own image and likeness;

- consider the questions they have about Jesus and where they could look for answers to those questions;
- apply Jesus' wisdom and example to current-day issues and situations.

Preparation

- Read and reflect on the second chapter of Matt Rawle's *Hollywood Jesus*.
- Read through this Leader Guide session in its entirety to familiarize yourself with the material being covered.
- Read and reflect on the following Scriptures:
  - ❑ Luke 17:11–19
  - ❑ John 9:1–17
  - ❑ Matthew 4:18–22
  - ❑ Matthew 8:23–27
  - ❑ Matthew 15:21–28
  - ❑ Luke 4:14–30
  - ❑ Luke 5:27–32
  - ❑ John 13:1–20
  - ❑ Jonah (the entire book)
- Make sure that you have a markerboard or large sheet of paper on which you can record group members' ideas.
- Have a Bible for every participant.
- Gather "Throwback Thursday" pictures from your participants, or arrange for them to bring in these pictures. Print these pictures or compile them in a slideshow. (For Opening Activity and Prayer.)
- Gather pictures of Jesus from a variety of sources. Print these pictures or compile them in a slideshow. (For an additional activity.)

Opening Activity and Prayer
(10–15 minutes)

Regardless of the day of the week on which you are meeting, celebrate "Throwback Thursday." At the time of this writing, Throwback Thursday is a social media phenomenon where users post pictures of themselves from an earlier time in their lives.

Before your session, ask participants to send you a Throwback Thursday picture of themselves. Print these out or compile them in a slideshow. (You also could have participants bring pictures with them.)

As a group, look at the pictures. For each one, discuss:

- When do you think this picture was taken? Where? What visual clues suggest when and where it was taken?
- What, if anything, surprises you about this picture?
- What does this picture tell you about the person depicted? What does it tell you about the time and place in which it was taken?
- Say something like: "While the biblical texts contain timeless truths, they also are products of a particular culture—a specific place and time. The same also is true of Hollywood portrayals of Jesus. Most of these movies reflect values, ideas, and issues from the cultures that created them, and many examine how Jesus' teaching and example apply to certain contemporary issues. As we look at the second chapter of *Hollywood Jesus*, we'll use movies to explore the relationship between Scripture and culture."

Lord, thank you for bringing us together again to explore connections between culture and the timeless truths of Jesus. Guide our study and our discussions that we can benefit from the wisdom of Scripture, writers and filmmakers, and one another. May we take what we learn during our time together and use it to more effectively tell Jesus' story to those who are eager to hear it or who need to hear it in new ways. Amen.

WATCH DVD SEGMENT
(10 MINUTES)

STUDY AND DISCUSSION
(30–35 MINUTES)

<u>Note:</u> Discussion helps and questions that correspond to Chapter Two: "The Jesus of Now…Whenever 'Now' Is" are provided below. If you have more time in your session, or want to include additional discussion and activities to your time, see "Additional Options for Bible Study and Discussion" at the end of this section, listed after the Closing Activity and Prayer.

Been-Hur
(See *Hollywood Jesus*, pages 48–52)

Read aloud or summarize for the group:

Matt Rawle uses the example of several Jesus movies, and particularly 1959s' *Ben-Hur,* to illustrate how the time and place in which a story is told affects how the teller chooses to tell it. *Ben-Hur's* good-guys-versus-bad-guys narrative would have made a lot of sense to Americans during the Cold War. Rawle points out that Jesus movies made in the 1970s shy away from absolutes that many people would have taken for granted less than twenty years earlier.

Activity:

Ask participants to think about stories that have been remade or updated. This could include books that are made into movies years after publication (such as *To Kill a Mockingbird)*, movies (such as *Ben-Hur, True Grit,* or *Ocean's Eleven*) that are remade, or stories that are rebooted for a new generation. Make a list of their examples. Choose two or three remakes, and ask:

- How did the remake differ from the original?
- How did both the original and the remake reflect the time, place, and culture in which they were created?

Then invite participants to take some time to consider how their images of Jesus have changed throughout their lifetimes and to identify what factors are responsible for these changes. Possible factors include maturity, greater knowledge of Scripture and its historical context, and a greater understanding of Christian theology.

Little Christs
(See *Hollywood Jesus*, pages 52–56)

Read aloud or summarize for the group:

Hollywood loves to take old stories and put them into modern-day settings. For example, filmmakers frequently create new takes on Shakespeare's plays, whether rewriting the story with current-day language and characters (such as 1999's *10 Things I Hate About You,* which was an update of *The Taming of the Shrew*) or using current-day elements when filming the original script (such as Baz Luhrmann's 1996 adaptation of

Romeo and Juliet). One might describe Shakespeare's stories as timeless. The same could be said of the stories in the Gospels.

Activity:

Read what Rawle has to say on page 55 about how *Jesus Christ Superstar* plays with the idea that, while Jesus lived in a particular place and time, he is timeless and still lives among us. *Superstar* takes place in Roman-controlled Judea, but characters drive cars and carry machine guns.

Divide participants into two teams and assign each team one of the following two Scriptures. (If you have a large number of participants, divide them into four teams and assign each Scripture to two teams.)

- Luke 17:11–19 (Keep in mind the intense animosity between Jews and Samaritans.)
- John 9:1–17

Each team should consider how a current-day filmmaker might approach its assigned Scripture. They should discuss the following questions:

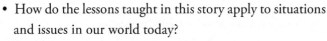

- How do the lessons taught in this story apply to situations and issues in our world today?
- What groups of people today might correspond to the groups of people mentioned in the Scripture? (Who would be the lepers? the Jews and Samaritans? the Pharisees?)

Allow teams about ten minutes to read their Scriptures and modernize their stories. Then have each team present its current-day rendering. Afterward, ask:

- How did our takes on these Scriptures show ways that the gospel is relevant in our twenty-first century world?
- What dangers are there in applying first-century Scriptures to a twenty-first century world?

Hero, Hippie, Clown, and Canadian
(See *Hollywood Jesus*, pages 57–59)

Read aloud or summarize for the group:

Rawle reminds us that Jesus "doesn't have just one face." Traditionally, the church has taught that Jesus works through the "offices" of king, prophet, priest, and servant. But Jesus' work is not limited to these traditional roles. We might also describe Jesus as a teacher, healer, or friend.

Activity:

Read each of the following Scriptures and discuss the role Jesus plays in each one. If you're running short on time, choose three or four.)

- Matthew 4:18–22
- Matthew 8:23–27
- Matthew 15:21–28
- Luke 4:14–30
- Luke 5:27–32
- John 13:1–20

For discussion:

- Why is it important that Jesus plays so many different roles?

31

- Think of portrayals of Jesus in film. Which roles do film-makers seem to focus on the most? Are there roles Jesus plays that you would like to see explored more in movies? If so, which ones?
- Which role(s) Jesus plays do you relate to most?
- How can lifting up the many roles that Jesus plays help more people to relate to Jesus?

The Last Temptation of Hollywood Jesus
(See *Hollywood Jesus*, pages 65–68)

Activity:

Ask each participant to take a few minutes to write a paragraph describing Jesus, in his or her own words. They can focus on his physical appearance, his priorities, his work, and/or significance.

- Collect everyone's paragraphs and shuffle them. Read aloud each of the paragraphs, and have participants guess the author. Each time, ask:
- If you correctly guessed the author of this paragraph, what clues gave you an idea that it belonged to that person? If you were wrong, why did you guess the way you did?

Read aloud or summarize for the group:

Rawle writes, "It is so very tempting to create Jesus in our own image and likeness." It makes sense that each of us would have his or her own unique description of Jesus. We know that Jesus plays many roles and relates to us in different ways. But if we aren't careful, it's easy for us to project our personal desires and priorities onto Jesus. Instead of imitating Jesus, we try to make Jesus an imitation of us.

For discussion:

- When have you been tempted to "create Jesus in [your] own image and likeness"? When might you have been guilty of trying to mold Jesus into someone who shares your priorities or political views?
- How can we be sure that we are aligning ourselves with Jesus' priorities instead of trying to make Jesus align with ours?
- How can we get past our assumptions, and the assumptions of others, and truly get to know Jesus?

CLOSING ACTIVITY AND PRAYER
(10 MINUTES)

Divide participants into teams of three of four. Instruct each team to brainstorm a short list of contemporary issues that Jesus might be particularly concerned about (such as poverty or immigration or climate change). After teams have spent a few minutes brainstorming, have each team select one issue and ask, "What would Jesus say about [this issue]?"

Teams should come up with several statements about Jesus' possible views on the selected issue. (For example, if the issue were immigration, statements might include, "Jesus calls us to ignore national borders and immigration policies and welcome all people" or "Jesus wants us to show compassion but also to uphold the rule of law and make sure immigrants are going through the proper channels.")

Teams should evaluate each of these statements, asking:

- What evidence do we have that Jesus would take this stance?

- What evidence do we have that suggests he would not?
- What questions do you have about this issue or about Jesus' teaching and example that would give you a better understanding of how Jesus might respond to this issue?

After teams have had five minutes to work, ask each one to name the issue it chose, read two or three of the statements it came up with, go over some of evidence for and against each statement, and read some of the questions raised.

Following all of the team presentations, ask:

- What did you learn from this activity, and from this session in general, about how we apply Jesus' teaching and example to current-day issues and situations?
- What are some of the different roles that Jesus plays? Why is it important to recognize that Jesus plays these many roles?
- What dangers do we face when applying Jesus' life and teaching to a current-day situation? How can we avoid these pitfalls?

Lord, thank you once again for this time we've had together. Thank you for living among us as Jesus and relating to us in so many different ways. Grant us the wisdom to look to your life and example when making decisions about or taking stances on current-day issues. Watch over us in the coming week that we might be mindful of all the ways you guide us and enter our world. In the name of Jesus—king, priest, prophet, servant, teacher, healer, and friend—we pray. Amen.

ADDITIONAL OPTIONS FOR BIBLE STUDY AND DISCUSSION

Activity: Jesus' Photo Album
(10 minutes)

Beforehand, compile a variety of pictures of Jesus. These can include stills from movies in which an actor portrays Jesus, illustrations from children's Sunday school materials, depictions of Jesus by renowned painters and sculptors, or interesting images of Jesus that you find on Internet image sites. Print out these pictures or compile them in a slideshow.

Show or set out these pictures of Jesus. Ask participants to look carefully at these pictures and to identify:

- the picture they think most accurately depicts Jesus;
- the picture they think least accurately depicts Jesus;
- the most interesting depiction of Jesus.

Take a count of how many people consider each picture most accurate, least accurate, or most interesting. For every picture that gets votes for any of the three categories, ask volunteers to explain why they selected the picture for that category. When it comes to the most accurate and least accurate categories, ask participants to explain how they determined accuracy. Did they use clues from Scripture? Information about the first-century Jewish world? Also ask them to name any assumptions they've made about who Jesus is or what he looks like. Are these assumptions based in facts? If not, where might they have come from?

For discussion:

- Why is it important to be aware of the assumptions we make about Jesus?
- How can we test our assumptions to see if they have merit and are based on factual (or plausible) information?
- What assumptions have filmmakers made about Jesus? Which of these assumptions seem to be faithful to Scripture and/or grounded in factual information? Which seem suspect?
- What things can we safely assume about Jesus?

Activity: Mimicking Love, Grace, and Mercy (10 minutes)

Hollywood has shown us that some aspects of Jesus' life, ministry, and teaching are timeless. Other aspects of Jesus' life are specific to the first-century Roman-Jewish world. Divide a markerboard or large sheet of paper into two columns. Title one column "Timeless" and the other "Dated." In the "Timeless" column, list things about Jesus that have as much meaning for us today as they had in the first century, things that would come across even in a modernized version of Jesus' story. In the "Dated" column, list things about Jesus that are entirely products of the particular time and place in which he lived and are not things that a follower of Christ today would necessarily emulate (such as speaking Aramaic or walking as a means of interstate travel).

Ask:

- How do you determine if a quality of Jesus is timeless or something specific to the culture in which he lived?

Then focus on the "Timeless" list. Rawle says that following Christ means "mimicking the love, grace, and mercy Christ offers in whichever culture we find ourselves." Look at each item on the "Timeless" list, and talk about ways that a Christian in our culture today could mimic this quality of Jesus. Challenge each participant to commit to one new way of mimicking Jesus. As time permits, have participants pair off and tell their partners about their commitments. Encourage partners to hold one another accountable to their commitments during the coming weeks.

An Absurd Truth

(See *Hollywood Jesus*, pages 60–64)

For discussion:

Rawle cites Monty Python's *Life of Brian* as an example of an absurd and satirical take on Jesus' story that nonetheless conveys some important truths about faith. With that in mind, discuss:

- What movies (or television shows or books or other media) have you encountered that take a humorous, irreverent, or satirical look at Jesus?
- Which of these did you find funny? Which did you find offensive? Which, do you think, actually imparted meaningful wisdom about Jesus' life, teaching, and impact? Are there any that you found both offensive *and* insightful?

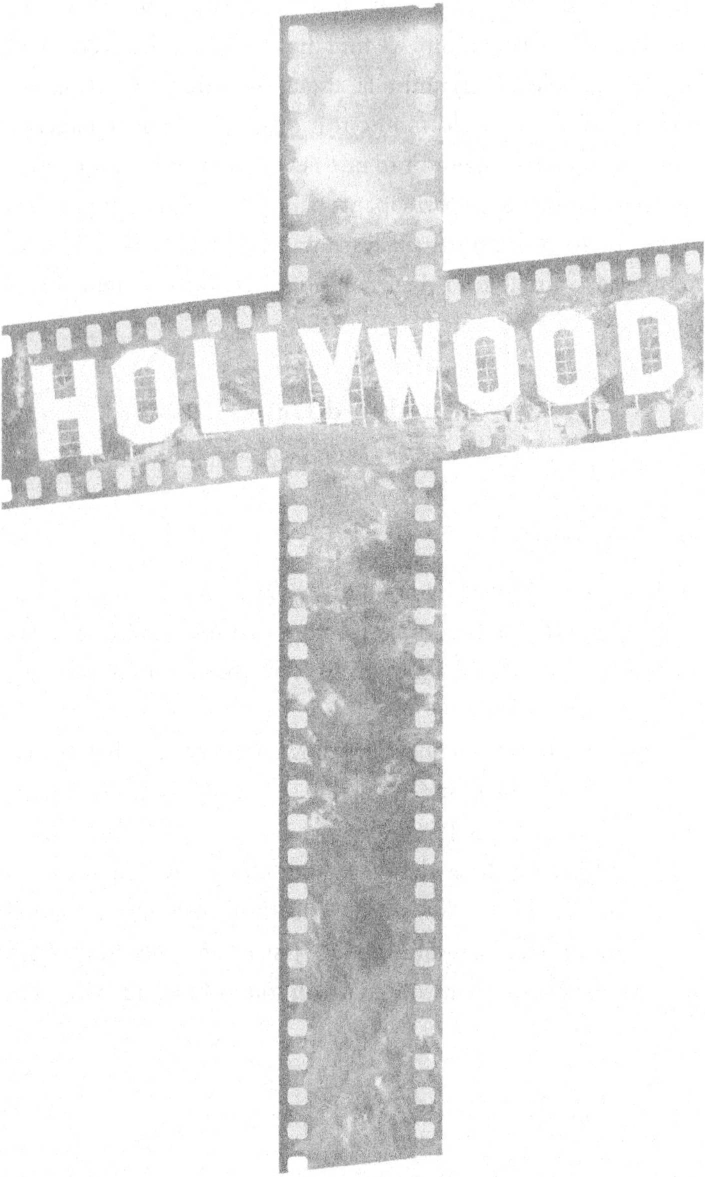
HOLLYWOOD

Session 3

THE GOSPEL ACCORDING TO . . .

PLANNING THE SESSION

Session Goals

Through this session's discussion and activities, participants will be encouraged to:

- consider how Christ is alive and at work, even in places where we would not expect to find him;
- look for glimpses of Jesus in our world today;
- remember their baptism (if they have been baptized) and who they are as a member of the body of Christ;
- determine ways that they can use elements of popular culture to communicate the gospel to those who are unfamiliar with it.

Preparation

- Read and reflect on the third chapter of Matt Rawle's *Hollywood Jesus*.

- Read through this Leader Guide session in its entirety to familiarize yourself with the material being covered.
- Read and reflect on the following Scriptures:
  - ❑ Genesis 22:1–19
  - ❑ Romans 7:15–20
  - ❑ Acts 17:17–34
- Make sure that you have a markerboard or large sheet of paper on which you can record group members' ideas.
- Have a Bible for every participant.
- Have paper and pens or pencils for every participant.
- Gather copies of your congregation or denomination's baptismal liturgy.

OPENING ACTIVITY AND PRAYER (10–15 MINUTES)

So far this study has focused on films in which Jesus is a primary character. This session looks at movies that, on their surface, have nothing to do with the person of Jesus, but nonetheless teach important truths about our faith.

To open your time together, have participants brainstorm movies that communicate Christian themes or virtues, even though you wouldn't find them in the "religion" section on Netflix. List these on a markerboard or large sheet of paper.

Brainstorm for a few minutes or until the ideas start to die down. Then go through the movies on your list and pick two or three, and ask participants to say what Christian message or idea each one conveys.

Ask:

- What do you think makes a movie a "Christian" movie?
- Look over the movies on our list. Do you think the filmmakers intended to include Christian ideas in their films?
- How could Christians embrace these movies and use them to teach the gospel?

Lord, thank you for bringing us back together to look at ways that Jesus is alive and at work in our world. We know that we serve a living Savior. Remind us of ways that you, in the person of Jesus and through the Holy Spirit, are living with us and among us. Guide our study and our discussions that we can benefit from the wisdom of Scripture, writers and filmmakers, and one another. Amen.

WATCH DVD SEGMENT (10 MINUTES)

STUDY AND DISCUSSION (30–35 MINUTES)

<u>Note:</u> Discussion helps and questions that correspond to Chapter Three: "The Gospel According to . . ." are provided below. If you have more time in your session, or want to include additional discussion and activities to your time, see "Additional Options for Bible Study and Discussion" at the end of this section, listed after the Closing Activity and Prayer.

From Jesus to Christ

(See *Hollywood Jesus*, pages 73–77)

Activity:

Rawle asks, "How do you lead people to Jesus when there is no Jesus to see?" We know that Jesus lives, but he is not among us in the flesh.

Divide participants into pairs or groups of three. Challenge each group to explain, in 30 seconds or less, how we see Jesus alive and at work in our world today. Give pairs and teams a couple of minutes to prepare, then have each team give its 30-second spiel. Then ask:

- What is one example of how Jesus is at work in the world today that you would not have thought of until someone in this group mentioned it?
- Should we speak of Jesus in the past tense, the present tense, or some combination of both? How do we determine when to say "is" and when to say "was"?
- Why is it important that we, as Christians, constantly look for evidence that Jesus is alive and among us? What is the danger of speaking about Jesus mostly in the past tense?

A Long Time Ago, in a Village Far, Far Away

(See *Hollywood Jesus*, pages 77–82)

For discussion:

In this chapter Rawle explores movies in which Jesus does not appear as a character but is still present. The "A Long Time Ago in a Village Far, Far Away" section examines Christian themes in the *Star Wars* saga. Ask:

- Rawle mentions several *Star Wars* characters who mirror Christ, either by their stories or by their wisdom and demeanor. In what other characters—whether in *Star Wars* or in other science fiction and fantasy epics—do you see Jesus?
- How, if at all, have such characters helped you better understand Jesus?
- How might these characters serve to introduce Jesus to people who are not familiar with him?

Read aloud or summarize for the group:

As Rawle notes, there are plenty of Christian parallels in the *Star Wars* series. He names several characters who have obvious similarities to Christ or who emulate what it means to be a follower of Christ—Anakin and Luke Skywalker, both of whom play almost messianic roles in the films, and Yoda and Obi-Wan Kenobi, whose wise teachings often echo those of Jesus. But Rawle also sees the gospel in the story of Han Solo—the brash smuggler, mercenary, and religious skeptic—as he learns how to respond to love.

For discussion:

- Science fiction and fantasy epics are full of Christlike characters. Invite participants to reflect on their favorite sci-fi and fantasy stories and the characters from these stories who most reflect Christ or illustrate what it means to follow Christ.

- Go around the group. Have each person name one sci-fi or fantasy character in whom they see Christ or the gospel and explain why he or she chose that character. Then ask:
- What is the value in looking for Christ or examples of Christ-like living in the stories and characters we enjoy?

Remember Who You Are
(See *Hollywood Jesus*, pages 93–97)

Activity:

In *The Lion King*, the young lion Simba must remember and reclaim his true identity, which reminds us of baptism in Christ. Those who have been baptized into the body of Christ must do the same and remember to whom we belong.

Beforehand gather copies of your denomination or congregation's baptismal liturgy. (This may be found in a hymnal or official denominational book, or even online.) Read through the baptismal vows, then ask:

- Is there anything you noticed in our church's baptismal vows that you hadn't before?
- When someone joins the Christian community through baptism, what commitments is he or she making (or are his or her parents making on his or her behalf?
- If you have been baptized, what, if anything, do you remember about your baptism? (If you were baptized as an infant, what have you been told about your baptism?)
- How frequently have you revisited the commitments you made, or those that were made for you, at your baptism?
- How do these vows remind us of who we are as members of the body of Christ?

44

CLOSING ACTIVITY AND PRAYER
(10–15 MINUTES)

To close your time together, revisit the list of movies you created as part of the opening activity. Cross out any movies that you discussed during this lesson. Then ask each participant to select one of the remaining films. Have each person name the movie he or she chose. Group together any participants who have chosen the same movie.

Instruct individuals to reflect on or teams to discuss the following questions:

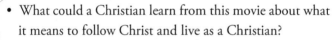

- What could a Christian learn from this movie about what it means to follow Christ and live as a Christian?
- What could a non-Christian learn from this movie about who Jesus is and what it means to be a Christian?
- How might our group or congregation use this movie to teach people about Jesus or living as Jesus' followers?

Allow individuals and teams a few minutes to reflect on these questions. Then ask each person or team to name the movie he, she, or they chose and to go over their answers to the questions. After every person or team has had a chance to talk, ask:

- What have you learned from this session about using movies—particularly those that we wouldn't describe as "Christian"—to communicate truths about Christ and the Christian faith?
- What movies will you see in a new light as a result of our discussions today?
- How might you approach movies, and other elements of popular culture, differently as a result of this session?

Lord, thank you once again for our time together. Thank you for living among us as Jesus, and thank you for living among us still today in the persons of Jesus and the Holy Spirit. Open our eyes to ways that you are at work in our lives and culture, even in places where we wouldn't expect to see you. Guide us as we make connections between faith and popular culture and as we look for ways to teach and demonstrate eternal gospel truths. Amen.

ADDITIONAL OPTIONS FOR BIBLE STUDY AND DISCUSSION

There and Back Again (10-15 minutes)
(See *Hollywood Jesus*, pages 87–92)

Activity:

In his treatment of *The Lord of the Rings* saga, Rawle looks at Genesis 22:1–19, often referred to as "The Binding of Isaac." Divide participants into three teams. One team should read these verses from Abraham's point of view. A second team should read the Scripture from Isaac's point of view. The third should read it from the point of view of Sarah, Isaac's mother and Abraham's wife, who isn't actually mentioned in this Scripture. (The third group will have to speculate about how much Sarah knew and when she might have known it.)

Give teams plenty of time to read and discuss, then have each team summarize the Scripture from its character's point of view, speculating about what its character might have been thinking.

Then ask:

- How did looking at this story from different points of view affect your understanding and appreciation of the story? What new questions did it raise?
- What do you find challenging or troubling about this Scripture?
- What do you think is the primary message or lesson of this Scripture?

Read aloud or summarize for the group:

While there are all sorts of takeaways from Genesis 22:1–19, on some level it shows Abraham's full and unwavering devotion to God. The Lord of the Rings trilogy tells the story of Frodo Baggins' full devotion to a quest to destroy a powerful ring in the fires of Mount Doom. What Frodo is asked to do is nearly as harrowing as what Abraham is asked to do. He must risk his life on a nearly impossible quest, all the while carrying an object that tempts him with the promise of unspeakable power.

Even when Frodo gets to Mount Doom, he struggles to cast it into the fire. The temptation to hold on to it is so strong that it nearly keeps Frodo from fulfilling his quest.

For discussion:

- What is "the ring" in your life? Why do you find difficult to let go?
- How does "the ring" in your life keep you from being fully devoted to God?
- What steps can you take in the coming week to rid yourself of your "ring"?

Activity: To an Unknown God
(15 minutes)

For discussion:

The apostle Paul obviously didn't have movies to use as a teaching tool, but he was nonetheless able to use elements of popular culture to teach truths about Christ.

Read aloud Acts 17:17–34, and ask:

- Why does Paul become "deeply distressed" while he waits for his companions in Athens?
- How does Paul end up spending his days in Athens?
- Based on this Scripture, how would you describe the religion of the Athenians? Do you think they would have been receptive to Christianity? Why, or why not?
- Reread verses 23 and 28. How does Paul use elements of Greek culture to teach the Athenians about Christ?
- What is the result of Paul's teaching?

You might point out that, when Paul tells the Athenians that they are "religious in every way," it probably isn't a compliment. Paul may be saying, sarcastically, "Wow. Look at all these idols. You guys must be *really* religious." The poem Paul cites in verse 28 may have been written by the third century B.C. Greek poet Aratus. Similar words are found in a poem by Cleanthes, one of Aratus's contemporaries. The phrase "In God we live, move, and exit" in verse 28 may be citing a poem by the ancient Greek philosopher Epimenides. At any rate, Paul in this Scripture is citing Greek pagan poets and philosophers to introduce his audience to Christ.

If time permits, divide participants into teams of four or five and have each team rewrite Acts 17:17–34, setting it in your city (or the nearest city to you). Teams do not need to do a complete word-for-word rewrite, but they should replace Paul with a current-day person, perhaps one of the members of the group; they should consider what idols are prominent in cities today (idols to gods such as money, power, vanity, and so forth); and they should replace Paul's references to Greek culture with references to American culture. (Instead of citing ancient poems, they might refer to popular songs that many Americans would be familiar with.)

After teams have had about five minutes to work, invite each team to read aloud the changes made to the Scripture. Ask:

- What can Christians today learn from Paul about using popular culture, including movies, as a tool for teaching Christ to those who are not familiar with him?

(A) Your Move – 4 Questions to Ask when you don't know What to do (Andy Stanley) — Making decisions

(B) Power of a Whisper Hearing God's still small voice & Responding (Bill Hybels)

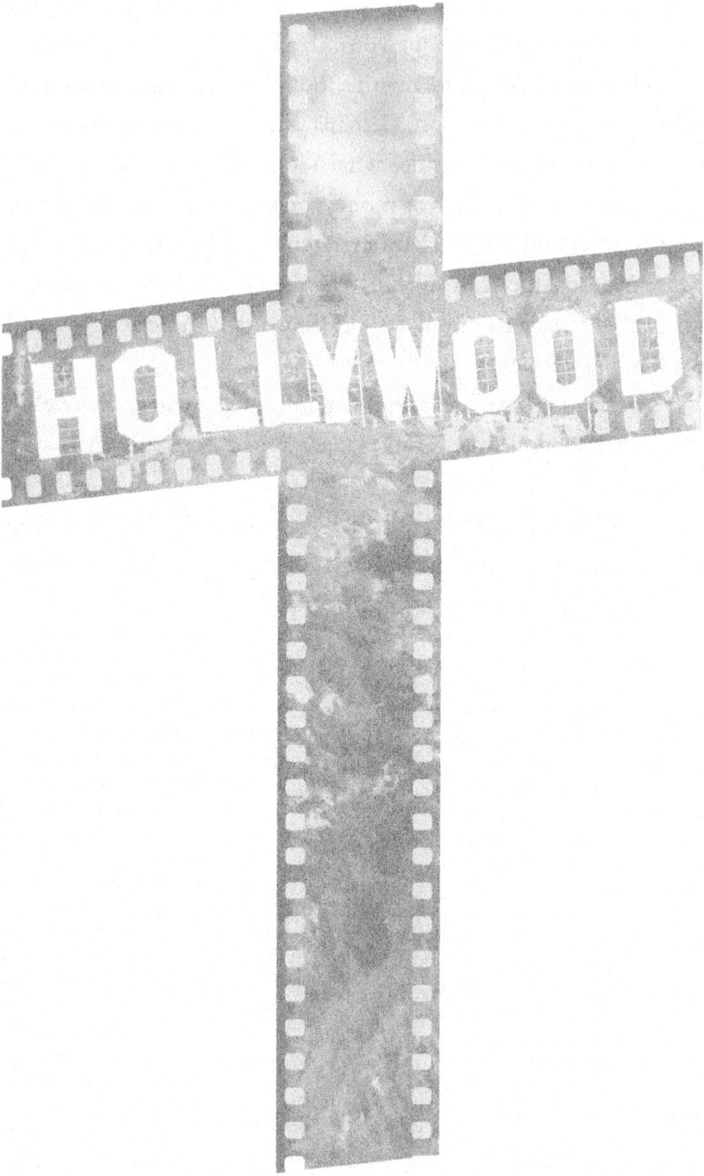
HOLLYWOOD

Session 4

EVERYONE HAS A STORY

PLANNING THE SESSION

Session Goals

Through this session's discussion and activities, participants will be encouraged to:

- examine what it means to serve a God who creates something out of nothing;
- affirm that all things are possible through God;
- identify ways that they, as a group and as members of a congregation, can create something from nothing, responding to needs in their community;
- consider what it means to become like children and have a childlike faith;
- tell their faith stories and consider what their story can teach others about Christ;

- reflect on film as a tool that Christians can use to spread the gospel message and grow in their understanding of God.

Preparation

- Read and reflect on the fourth chapter of Matt Rawle's *Hollywood Jesus.*
- Read through this Leader Guide session in its entirety to familiarize yourself with the material being covered.
- Read and reflect on the following Scriptures:
  - ❏ Matthew 5:38–42
  - ❏ Matthew 19:16–26
  - ❏ Genesis 3
  - ❏ Matthew 18:1–5
  - ❏ Ephesians 1:15–19
- Make sure that you have a markerboard or large sheet of paper on which you can record group members' ideas.
- Have a Bible, for every participant.
- Have paper and pens or pencils for every participant.

OPENING ACTIVITY AND PRAYER
(10–15 MINUTES)

Open your final session together by asking participants to reflect on these two questions:

- What one movie best describes or illustrates your relationship with and experience of Christ?
- If you were to make a movie to teach an important truth about God or about following Christ, what kind of movie would it be? What would the plot be? Who would it star?

Give participants a few minutes to think over their answers then go around the room and have each person name the movie he or she chose and explain the movie he or she would make.

Lord, thank you for bringing us back together for this final session. Bless our time together as we continue to explore the ways that you speak to us through film. Open our eyes, ears, and hearts that we may learn and grow in our faith through Scripture, art, culture, and the wisdom and witness of one another. We pray this in the name of Jesus of Hollywood and of all times and places. Amen.

WATCH DVD SEGMENT
(10 MINUTES)

STUDY AND DISCUSSION
(30–35 MINUTES)

<u>Note:</u> Discussion helps and questions that correspond to Chapter Four: "Everyone Has a Story" are provided below. If you have more time in your session, or want to include additional discussion and activities to your time, see "Additional Option for Bible Study and Discussion" at the end of this section, listed after the Closing Activity and Prayer.

Sometimes Nothing Can Be a Real Cool Hand
(See *Hollywood Jesus*, pages 103–106)

Activity:

Divide participants into teams of three or four and challenge each team to sketch out a plan for a party. Here's the catch:

Your party will be in an empty room containing nothing but a chair for each person attending. There is nothing else in the room, and partygoers may not bring anything with them. In other words, teams must plan a party using nothing.

Allow teams a few minutes to plan their parties. Then ask each team to explain its party to the others. After all of the teams have presented their plans, vote on which party sounds like the most fun. Congratulate groups on their creativity and ability to bring something out of nothing.

For discussion:

Scholars and theologians sometimes refer to God's creation of the cosmos as *creation ex nihilo*, meaning "creation from nothing." Why do you think it's important to say that God created from nothing, instead of just saying that God created?

- Often *creation ex nihlio* refers to how God created all things in the beginning, but it doesn't have to be so specific. How does God still bring something out of nothing? How has God brought something out of nothing in your life?
- What does God's ability to bring something from nothing tell us about God?
- Look over what Rawle has to say about *Cool Hand Luke* in this chapter of *Hollywood Jesus*. How does Luke in these examples make something out of seemingly nothing?
- Read Matthew 5:38–42. How does *Cool Hand Luke* illustrate Jesus' teaching in these verses?

The Gospel According to You

(See *Hollywood Jesus*, pages 119–122)

For discussion:

- Read aloud Ephesians 1:15–19. In these verses, the apostle Paul prays for the Christians in Ephesus, that the "eyes of [their] heart will have enough light to see what is the hope of God's call." When and how have you been aware of God's call?
- At this point in your life, are you aware of a particular calling or purpose that God has set in front of you? If so, what is it?
- If you do have a sense of calling or purpose, how has God equipped you to fulfill this calling? What gifts and resources has God given you?

Activity: *How can you find meant of how?*

Note: Be aware that this could be a lengthy activity. Plan to spend 20–25 minutes on this activity alone.

Challenge participants to imagine that they are creating a movie about their life. Make sure that each person has paper and something to write with. Each participant should come up with:

- A title
- A list of main characters
- A summary of the plot
- A tagline that could be used to promote the movie (something for posters and commercials)

As they map out their movies, participants should consider the following questions. (You might write these on a markerboard or large sheet of paper so participants can refer back to them often.)

- What role will your faith play in this movie?
- What conflict(s) will drive the plot?
- What might viewers learn from the way you respond to this conflict?
- What might viewers learn about God from your movie?
- What might they learn about what it means to follow Christ?

Give participants about 10 minutes to work. Then divide them into teams of three or four and have teams discuss their autobiographical movie ideas, including the questions above. After teams have had a few minutes to talk, ask:

- Who in your team (other than yourself) had a particularly interesting movie idea?
- What truths about Christ and Christian living would this movie convey?

CLOSING ACTIVITY AND PRAYER (10–15 MINUTES)

To close, challenge participants to name as many movies as they can that they have mentioned or discussed during this study. List all of these movies on a markerboard or large sheet of paper. Ask each participant to write down the top three movies he or she thinks best communicate a truth about Christ and our relationship with Christ.

Go through the list, and as each movie title is read, ask participants to raise their hands if the movie was in his or her top-3 list. For each vote, make tally marks next to the movie title. When all the movie titles have been read, circle the top five with the most votes.

For each movie on the top-5 list, discuss:

- If you had to summarize the Christian message of this movie in one word, what word would you use?
- What truth(s) about Christ does this movie communicate?
- How might the church use this movie as a teaching tool? Whom might the church be able to reach with this movie who wouldn't be reached otherwise?

Wrap up the entire series with the following questions. You can discuss these questions as a group, have participants pair off and discuss these questions with a partner, or divide participants into small teams for discussion.

- What is one thing you learned from this study that you didn't know before?
- What is one thing you learned from or about one of the other participants that has had a positive impact on your faith or relationship with Christ?
- What is one movie that you look at or interpret differently as a result of this study?
- What makes movies an effective tool for teaching the gospel message, either as a congregation or as individuals?
- In what ways might our group or congregation use movies to introduce people to Christ?
- In what ways might our group or congregation use movies to enhance our understanding of God and Christian theology?

Lord, thank you for bringing us together for the past few weeks. Thank you for all the ways that you speak to us and teach us, including through the movies. Thank you for the witness of our fellow participants, for their wisdom, and for their stories. Watch over us as we go from here that we may apply the lessons we've learned and that we may find creative ways to use art and popular culture to spread the gospel message and grow in our faith and our relationship with you. We pray in the name of the one who lived among us in the flesh and continues to be manifest among us in many ways, including on the big screen. Amen.

ADDITIONAL OPTIONS FOR BIBLE STUDY AND DISCUSSION

A Monstrous Fear (10 minutes)
(See *Hollywood Jesus*, pages 115–119)

Activity:

Go around the room and ask each person to name a movie that he or she loved as a child. Each participant also should name something he or she loved about the movie when he or she was young and something that he or she appreciates about the movie as an adult but wouldn't have noticed as a child.

For discussion:

- Read aloud Genesis 3:1–13. What happened to the man and woman's understanding of the world as a result of the events in this chapter?

- How is Adam and Eve's experience in this chapter similar to what we all go through as we transition from childhood to adulthood?
- Rawle writes in this chapter that "love was transformed into fear"? Why were Adam and Eve afraid? What were they afraid of?
- Rawle adds that, through Christ, God transforms fear into love. How has Christ helped you transform or overcome your fears?

Activity:

Rawle uses the Pixar classic *Monsters, Inc.* to address the topic of fear. Ask participants to name one or two other children's movies that teach important lessons about responding to fear. For each movie named, ask:

- What does this movie teach us about our relationship with Christ?
- Read aloud Matthew 18:1–5. Why does Jesus instruct us to become like children?
- How do we become like little children?
- What is the difference between becoming like children and being childish?
- How does becoming like children affect our relationship with God?
- How does being childlike affect how we love? How does it affect how we respond to fear?

59

Plastic Jesus (10–15 minutes)

(See *Hollywood Jesus*, pages 107–111)

Activity:

Read aloud Matthew 19:16–26. Jesus tells the rich man in these verses, "It's easier for a camel to squeeze through the eye of a needle than for a rich person to enter God's kingdom."

(Some participants in your group may have heard that Jesus could have been referring to a narrow gate in Jerusalem called the Needle's Eye or Eye of the Needle. This idea originated in the Middle Ages; there is no historical evidence that such a gate existed in first-century Jerusalem. It is most likely that Jesus was talking about an actual sewing needle.)

Have the group brainstorm other illustrations to suggest that something is impossible, or practically impossible. For example, "It is easier for a snowman to cross the Sahara desert . . . " or "It is easier for a moth to fly to Mars . . ." Compile your examples on a markerboard or large sheet of paper.

For discussion:

- Jesus wants his disciples to know that a rich person entering God's kingdom is, for all intents and purposes, impossible. But he doesn't leave things there. Reread verse 26.

- When you consider all of what Jesus says in these verses— what he says to the rich man, what he says about the camel and the needle, and what he says about all things being possible with God—what main point or points do you think Jesus is making? What does he want his listeners to take away from this exchange?

Taking the Red Pill (15 minutes)
(See *Hollywood Jesus*, pages 111–115)

Activity:

God created something out of nothing and gives us the ability to do the same. Rawle asks, "What in your community do you tend to think of as 'nothing' that God might be calling you to transform?" Where, particularly in our community, do you see a need that needs to be met or something that is missing?

Divide participants into teams of three or four and have the teams struggle with these questions by going through the following steps (which you might list on a markerboard or large sheet of paper):

- Identify a need in your community or something that is missing.
- Identify groups or ministries in your community that already are working to meet this need or fill this gap.
- Identify biblical or theological reasons to get involved in an effort to meet this need or fill this gap.
- Identify ways your group or congregation can work with existing ministries or organizations to meet this need or fill this gap.
- Identify new things that your group or congregation can do to meet this need or fill this gap.

Allow the teams about ten minutes to work through these steps. The second and third steps likely will require them to do a little research with their phones or electronic devices. Then have each team present its idea.

As a group commit to following through on one team's idea. Determine next steps and roles that need to be filled. At least one person will need to talk with your church's pastoral staff and any relevant committees. At least one person will need to contact the ministries and/or organizations that you would like to work with. You will need to determine needs such as supplies and facilities, and you will need to figure out how much money you will need to get started and where this money will come from.

Time may not permit you to get everything worked out. You may need to plan a follow-up meeting or make arrangements to continue planning over social media.

CPSIA information can be obtained at www.ICGtesting.com
Printed in the USA
LVOW04s1632100815

449281LV00004B/4/P